Mother G

A Pantomime

Verne Morgan

Samuel French - London
New York - Sydney - Toronto - Hollywood

© 1981 by Verne Morgan

This play is fully protected under the Copyright Laws of the British Commonwealth of Nations, the United States of America and all countries of the Berne and Universal Copyright Conventions.

All rights, including Stage, Motion Picture, Radio, Television, Public Reading, and Translation into Foreign Languages, are strictly reserved.

No part of this publication may lawfully be transmitted, stored in a retrieval system, or reproduced in any form or by any means, electronic, mechanical, photocopying, manuscript, typescript, recording, or otherwise, without the prior permission of the copyright owners.

Rights of Performance by Amateurs are controlled by SAMUEL FRENCH LTD, 26 SOUTHAMPTON STREET, LONDON WC2E 7JE, and they, or their authorized agents, issue licences to amateurs on payment of a fee. It is an infringement of the Copyright to give any performance or public reading of the play before the fee has been paid and the licence issued.

Licences are issued subject to the understanding that it shall be made clear in all advertising matter that the audience will witness an amateur performance; that the names of the authors of the plays shall be included on all announcements and on all programmes; and that the integrity of the author's work will be preserved.

The Royalty Fee indicated below is subject to contract and subject to variation at the sole discretion of Samuel French Ltd.

> Basic fee for each and every
> performance by amateurs   Code H
> in the British Isles

In Theatres or Halls seating Six Hundred or more the fee will be subject to negotiation.

In Territories Overseas the fee quoted above may not apply. A fee will be quoted on application to our local authorized agent, or if there is no such agent, on application to Samuel French Ltd, London.

The Professional Rights in this play are controlled by Samuel French Ltd.

ISBN 0 573 06461 X

CHARACTERS

Sheriff of Gooseland
Silly Willy, his assistant
Jill, who is Queen of the May
Jack, Mother Goose's son
A Goose-Called-Priscilla
Mother Goose, a woman with social aspirations
Tommy, a village youth
Squire Tawdry, a nasty piece of work
Gretchen, from Amsterdam
Marjorie, daughter of Squire Tawdry
Demon Cursemall (pronounced "curse 'em all")
Fairy Tinsel, an ethereal sprite
Father Christmas
A Headless Ghost
A Very Tall Ghost
King of Gooseland

Dancers, Choristers (Villagers of Gooseland),
brothers and sisters of Gretchen

ACT I
Scene 1   Village of Gooseland
Front cloth interlude
Scene 2   Boutique de Gander
Front cloth interlude
Scene 3   The Wishing Well Glade

ACT II
Scene 1   The Snow Mountains
Front cloth interlude
Scene 2   The Royal Court of Justice

The following statement concerning the use of music is printed here on behalf of the Performing Right Society Ltd, by whom it was supplied

The permission of the owner of the performing right in copyright music must be obtained before any public performance may be given, whether in conjunction with a play or sketch or otherwise, and this permission is just as necessary for amateur performances as for professional. The majority of copyright musical works (other than oratorios, musical plays and similar dramatico-musical works) are controlled in the British Commonwealth by the PERFORMING RIGHT SOCIETY LTD, 29–33 BERNERS STREET, LONDON W1P 4AA.

The Society's practice is to issue licences authorizing the use of its repertoire to the proprietors of premises at which music is publicly performed, or, alternatively, to the organizers of musical entertainments, but the Society does not require payment of fees by performers as such. Producers or promoters of plays, sketches, etc., at which music is to be performed, during or after the play or sketch, should ascertain whether the premises at which their performances are to be given are covered by a licence issued by the Society, and if they are not, should make application to the Society for particulars as to the fee payable.

Should producers require assistance with the choosing of songs for this pantomime, or helpful suggestions regarding staging and production, Verne Morgan will be pleased to hear from them. Please address letters to Verne Morgan, c/o Samuel French Ltd.

SONG PLOT

Act I

Song
1. Opening Number (to the tune of *Wonderful, Wonderful, Copenhagen*) — Company
2. Queen Of The May (to the tune of *Alice Blue Gown*) — Jill, Jack, Chorus and Dancers
3. Duet — Jack and Jill
4. Song — Gretchen, Children, Chorus and Dancers
5. Duet — Tommy and Marjorie
6. Finale Scene 1 — Company
7. Song (*optional*) — Fairy
8. Country Number — Chorus and Dancers
9. Song — Jack
10. Mother Goose Is In The Well (to the tune of the popular 16 bars from *Orpheus In The Underworld* invariably used for the Can Can) — Choristers

FOUR SEASONS INTERLUDE

Spring. To Mendelssohn's *Spring Song* — Chorus and Dancers
Summer. To *The Campbells Are Coming* — Willy, Sheriff, Chorus and Dancers
Autumn. To *John Peel* — Willy, Sheriff, Chorus and Dancers
Winter. To *Auld Lang Syne* — Willy, Sheriff, Chorus and Dancers

11. Song — Mother Goose
12. Production Number — Company

Act II

13	Snowman Mime/Song	Dancers, Chorus and Children
14	Comedy Duet	Willy and Sheriff
15	Duet	Tommy and Marjorie
16	Comedy Duet	Mother Goose and Squire
17	Speciality	Gretchen
18	Duet	Jack and Jill
18a	Skeleton Dance (*optional*)	Dancers
19	Duet	Gretchen and Squire
20	Community Chorus Song (with song sheet)	Mother Goose, Willy and Sheriff
21	Ensemble Number	Principals and Chorus
21a	Speciality Dance	Dancers
21b	March Down	Company
22	Finale (reprise of popular number)	Company

This Music Plot does not include any incidental music which might be needed.

A Licence issued by Samuel French Ltd to perform this pantomime does not include permission to perform any copyright songs or music. Please read carefully the note supplied by the Performing Right Society

COSTUME SUGGESTIONS

The **Choristers** are dressed as Villagers, girls in bell-shaped skirts worn over petticoats, and frilly caps.
The men are in rustic attire.
The **Dancing Ladies** are dressed similarly, but have more of a schoolgirl appeal. They change as often as the budget will allow, plus of course speciality make-ups for things like The Four Seasons and the last scene.
The **Children** are dressed traditionally Dutch, but can change for Act II.
Jack commences as a poor boy so the costume should be modest, but well-elaborated after scene 2, when he becomes rich.
Jill, as Queen of the May, should be in white. After which as many changes as desirable.
Marjorie, being the Squire's daughter, should be pretty and smart.
Gretchen is traditional Dutch throughout.
Mother Goose wears the traditional pannier dress with mob-cap until she becomes rich. After that, anything "way-out" is permissible.
The rest of the cast are obvious.
The **Fairy** should always wear white, and the **Demon** red.
Priscilla-the-Goose should be an attractive and pretty bird, preferably played by a young dancer.
Headless Ghost A frame is stretched across the man's real head over which the jacket is placed, giving the illusion of being headless. It is advisable to cast a man of rather short stature to give credibility.
Very Tall Ghost The effect is achieved by a person carrying a long pole on which is attached a head plus a very long white sheet which reaches to the ground, completely covering the man underneath.

The Four Seasons Episode on page 27 is a full production number in four complete sections, each section segues to the next without pause.

Dancers. Sets of four can be used, i.e. a different troupe for each season, in which case each set are dressed accordingly. Alternatively, if one troupe only is used throughout they can be dressed in leotards or white ballet frocks, with suitable embellishments attached, including head-dresses, to represent the season as the occasion arises.

Music for Dances. The music of the preceding number can be used if found suitable, or a dance number interpolated according to the choreographer's wishes, or a mixture of both. Bearing in mind it is a long item, the dances should be kept reasonably short, and as much mime as possible should be introduced.

N.B. The poetical love-making of Gretchen and the Squire should be "ham acted", i.e. very exaggerated.

ACT I

Scene 1

The Village of Gooseland

It is representative of the village green. Shops and period houses can be included in the surround. In the foreground is Mother Goose's cottage, opposite is The Inside Inn. A village pump and other trappings can be instituted at the producer's direction

As the Curtain *rises, the Choristers, dressed in bright village costumes, are strolling about singing the opening number. There is an air of gaiety and careless abandon*

SONG 1: **Gooseland Wonder**

Chorus Come t' the, Come t' the
Gooseland wonder,
Magic is there in the sky,
You'll find lots to do,
And there's fairies too,
You can get there if you try.
Wonderful, wonderful Gooseland wonder,
Ev'rything spoken in rhyme,
We will introduce
You to Mother Goose,
You'll be filled with wonder,
Wonderful wonder and
Have a wonderful time!

As the chorus is repeated, the Dancers enter and take the stage

The Choristers continue the vocal. At the end of the number the Dancers and Choristers fan out, leaving the centre free for the Sheriff's entrance

The Sheriff enters

Sheriff 'Morning all.
All Good morning, Sheriff.

Sheriff As you know, today is May Day.
All Yes! Yes!
Sheriff Our folk-festival is now about to begin, and very shortly we will go through the ceremony of crowning our May Queen.
All Hurrah!
Sheriff The Squire will be here any moment for the purpose of choosing the most comeliest among you for the job.
All Aaah!
Sheriff So off you go now, and all you females make yourselves look as pretty as you can.

There is general hubbub and excitement as the chorus of SONG 1 *is reprised*

Everybody, including the Sheriff, exits. Silly Willy enters. He is a yokel, and wears a large soft hat with a dent in the crown. He trots down stage and addresses the audience

Willy Hallo! Are you sitting comfortably? Are you? I wish I was! D'you know something? Last night I dreamt I was wide awake, and when I woke up I found myself fast asleep! So I went back to bed again. I bet you don't know who I am. Shall I tell you? I'm Willy! They call me *Silly* Willy, because I'm such a silly-Billy! I bet you all thought I was the May Queen, didn't you? I bet you did! Oh yes you did! D'you know something? Folks all think I'm daft, but 'tween you and me—I'm not as daft as they think I am. Last night my mother sent me to the *Inside Inn* to get her a jug of beer. But she forgot to give me a jug. So I says to the landlord, "Not to worry, I'll take the beer in my hat." (*He removes his hat and turns it upside down, holding it at arm's length in the manner of a jug*). He fills my hat with beer, and then he says, "There's a little drop left over Willy, where will you have that, in your pocket?" He thinks I'm daft y'see! But I outwitted him, "No," I says, "I've got a dent in my hat t'other side, I'll take the rest in that." And I turns my hat over like this. (*He turns the hat over so that the crown-with-the-dent is now uppermost*) Then I walks home very careful-like, making sure not to spill none, and when I got inside the house my mother says, "Is that all the beer you got?" "No, Mum," I says, "the rest of it's *in here!*" (*He turns the hat over again*) Have you all got a handkerchief? Will you take it out of your pocket and hold it up high like this. (*He takes a handkerchief out of his pocket and holds it aloft in his right hand*) If you haven't got a handkerchief hold your programme up. If you haven't got a programme just hold your right hand

Act I, Scene 1 3

up. That's it! Now wave your hands from right to left, like this. That's it, go on—wave! Keep waving! Good-bye! Good-bye!

Willy exits, waving his handkerchief

The music strikes up immediately for the next number as the Choristers and Dancers enter. Four Chorus men are carrying a throne-chair which they are supporting by two poles laid across their shoulders. In the chair is Jill. She has just been crowned Queen of the May and is wearing her crown.

The Dancers dance in front of and around her as the Choristers sing—

SONG 2 Queen of the May

All   Now we've crowned you the Queen of the May,
You're the happiest girl of the day,
You look so proud and shy, As you catch ev'ry eye,
And your crown gaily glitters
When you're passing by,
Ev'rybody's so happy today,
'Tis a crown you are proud to display,
It does something for you,
We'll always adore you,
Our dear little Queen of the May.

The chorus is repeated and the Dancers elaborate the dance

  During the dance Jack enters

Jack stands entranced, unable to take his eyes off Jill. As the chorus nears its finish and everyone makes to exit Jack steps forward, takes Jill by the hand as the throne-chair is lowered, and solo's the last few bars

  All exit as Jack sings

Jack (*solo*) It does something for you,
             I'll always adore you,
             My dear little Queen of the May.

The stage is now clear except for Jack and Jill

    (*Overwhelmed*) You look just wonderful!
Jill Sir, you're a flatterer!
Jack The loveliest May Queen that ever was.

Jill Who are you?
Jack My name is Jack. I'm Mother Goose's son.
Jill My name is Jill.
Jack Yes, I know.
Jill Do you?
Jack Yes, we've met before.
Jill Have we?
Jack Many times. In my dreams!

SONG 3

Jack and Jill exit after their duet and immediately we hear a tremendous commotion off, shouting and yelling, etc. The orchestra picks up with some suitable music which rises to a crescendo as the Goose enters. She is chased on by the Villagers. They attack her with sticks and some pretend to kick her. Others throw their hat at her, all the while shouting, "Kick it!" "Kill it!" "Chase it!" ad lib., as they surround her and pummel into her. The door of Mother Goose's cottage opens, and Mother Goose enters. She takes in the scene in a trice. She then wades into the scrum hitting out left, right, and centre

Mother Goose Cut it out! You brutes! You monsters! Take *that*! And that! And that!

The Villagers make a hurried and undignified exit, Mother Goose going for them until the last one has gone

Mother Goose then sinks to a sitting posture, completely exhausted after her exertions. She sits on her doorstep fanning herself with her apron, and breathing heavily. The music stops. The Goose watches her from a safe distance. She too is exhausted, and limping badly

Oh dear, oh dear, oh dear!

The Goose plucks up courage and timorously advances towards her, unnoticed by Mother Goose. She rubs her beak up and down Mother Goose's back, very tenderly and very slowly

(*Jumping up*) What's that? What's that? (*She faces the Goose with her arms in a fighting position. Then realizes her mistake and relaxes*) Oh, it's you! I thought it was the Squire, getting fresh! (*She sits again*)

The Goose nestles its beak in her lap

Act I, Scene 1

(*Caressing her*) Oh, isn't she beautiful? How could anyone be cruel to her?

The Goose moves c, and mother Goose follows. Suddenly the Goose turns and raises its beak to Mother Goose's face

Oh look! She wants to kiss me! (*She kisses the Goose on the beak.*) Pooh! She must have eaten fried worms for breakfast! Tell me, Goosey, what's your name?

The Goose becomes very coy, and drops her head

Come on, don't be shy.

The Goose squirms, and sways in an embarrassed way

Well, whisper it then!

Mother Goose lowers her head and the Goose whispers into her ear

Is it? Really? (*To the audience*) She says her name is Priscilla!

The Goose motions Mother Goose to lower her head again, which she does

You want to know *my* name? Well, everyone knows me! I'm Mother Goose!

The Goose faces her and executes an enormous curtsy. Mother Goose replies with an even bigger curtsy, and nearly falls over

Priscilla, tell me, are you lost?

The Goose nods its head sadly

Oh dear! Where are you going to spend the night?

The Goose runs towards her and snuggles itself under her arm

(*Horrified*) With me? Oh dear! I'd love to have you, but you see, my house is very small, and I'm very poor.

The Goose walks sadly away and begins to cry

(*To the audience*) Isn't she sweet? Shall I take her in? Shall I?

As the audience shout their reply the Goose pops her head up and listens. Then cries again copiously

Oh dear! I don't know what to do. Priscilla, come here and dry your eyes. (*She brings forth a large handkerchief from somewhere down in her bosom*) Come on! (*She dabs Priscilla's eyes*) Now stop being such a silly Goose! Blow!

The Goose takes an enormous intake of breath and blows her nose into the handkerchief very noisily. Mother Goose holds the handkerchief up disclosing a large hole in the centre of it

Tell you what we'll do, poor or not poor, you shall come and live with me!

The orchestra strikes up a lively six-eight jig, something in the character of "The Irish Washerwoman", Mother Goose and Priscilla face each other and go into a short robust little dance, whirling round each other, bobbing and scraping, and lifting high their knees

Mother Goose and the Goose exit, still dancing, into Mother Goose's cottage. Tommy enters, followed by the Squire

Squire (*breathlessly*) Hi! Young man, I want a word with you.
Tommy Oh, hallo, Squire.
Squire What's this I hear about you?
Tommy What do you hear about me?
Squire That you are chatting up my daughter, Marjorie!
Tommy Oh Squire, we're in love!
Squire In love? With my daughter? You are just a village lad, you've no money and no prospects.
Tommy But I'll word hard sir, if only I can get a job.
Squire You would? (*Sizing him up*) Hmm! How would you like to work for me?
Tommy What as?
Squire As a "wife-sitter".
Tommy A "wife-sitter"? You mean a baby-sitter.
Squire No, a wife-sitter! Listen, listen! I'll let you into a little secret. I've been advertizing for an *au pair* girl.
Tommy An *au pair* girl?
Squire Yes, to do odd jobs about the house.
Tommy I see.
Squire Well, I've got one coming right now, on her way from Amsterdam.
Tommy A little Dutch girl eh?
Squire Yes, a Dutch girl. And I'm willing to pay someone to sit with my wife while I sit and pay attention to the *au pair* girl. Get me?
Tommy I do indeed.
Squire Will you do it?
Tommy Well, it's against all my principles ...

Act I, Scene 1   7

Squire Is it? Well I'm against your principle of courting my daughter Marjorie.

Off, there is much shouting accompanied by wolf-whistles, and the orchestra strike up a few bars of "I've seen Diamonds in Amsterdam"

Tommy (*looking off*) What's that?
Squire It is! It's my little Dutch girl! What's your name boy?
Tommy Tommy.
Squire Tommy, will you do it?
Tommy Yes.
Squire (*jumping about with excitement*) Then start your duties Tommy, go to my house and start your duties. (*Sentimentally*) I want to be alone!

Tommy exits. Gretchen enters. She is dressed in traditional Dutch costume

Gretchen (*as the music stops*) Hallo everybody! I'm Gretchen!
Squire Hallo Gretchen! I'm Squire Tawdry, your new boss.
Gretchen You're not!
Squire I am!
Gretchen Ha, ha, ha!
Squire What's so funny?
Gretchen Your face.
Squire What's the matter with my face?
Gretchen Is it the only one you've got?
Squire Of course it's the only one I've got.
Gretchen I thought perhaps you were trying it out for somebody.
Squire Now look here my good girl ...
Gretchen How do *you* know I'm a good girl?
Squire (*hopefully*) Aren't you then?
Gretchen *That* you'll have to find out, old fuzzy face.
Squire Fuzzy face?
Gretchen But then, you're too old to be interested no doubt.
Squire No! No I'm not too old, honestly!
Gretchen We'll see!
Squire Remember there's many a good fiddle played on an old tune; I mean, there's many a a good violin—that is to say, there's many a good fiddle—in fact there's thousands of 'em.
Gretchen I'm hungry.
Squire Of course you are! After your long journey you must be starving.

Gretchen We're all starving.
Squire All? Who's all?
Gretchen My little brothers and sisters.
Squire (*aghast*) Your brothers and sisters? Don't tell me you've brought 'em all with you!
Gretchen Yes, you'll love 'em. (*She calls*) Come on kids! Come and meet your new daddy!
Squire *Daddy?*

Several Children enter. They also are dressed in traditional Dutch, half as boys half as girls. They race on surrounding the Squire shouting:—"Daddy! Daddy! Hallo, dear Daddy!" etc., as they cling to him, and one small one jumps up into his arms

Hey! Get off! Get off! (*He pushes them angrily away*) Get out of it, you forward little hussies. Scram!
Gretchen Oh Squire, don't be cross. They've been learning a little song coming over on the boat, to sing to you on arrival.
Squire Have they? Well they can sing it to themselves, I'm going home to my wife.

The Squire exits hurriedly

SONG 4

They all exit after the number. Tommy enters

Tommy Dear oh dear oh dear! There's no pleasing the Squire. "I want you to pay attention to my wife" he says, and I was no sooner doing it than in he comes and kicks me out! Maybe I'm using the wrong after-shave! Anyhow, it's going to be tough, working for the Squire. Still, it may mean I shall see more of Marjorie.

Marjorie enters

Marjorie Tommy!
Tommy Marjorie!
Marjorie Where are you going?
Tommy I was thinking of going into the *Inside Inn*.
Marjorie What for?
Tommy To drown my sorrows.
Marjorie What sorrows?
Tommy The Squire's just given me a job.
Marjorie The Squire? You mean—my father?

Act I, Scene 1

Tommy Unfortunately—yes!
Marjorie What's so unfortunate about it?
Tommy If I tell you, you'll never believe me.
Marjorie Try me. I'll do my best!
Tommy Well, your father's given me a job looking after your mother.
Marjorie I beg your pardon?
Tommy While he, nasty old man, looks after Gretchen.
Marjorie Who's Gretchen?
Tommy Your new *au pair*.
Marjorie I don't believe it.
Tommy It's true.
Marjorie Father wouldn't do such a thing.
Tommy I know he's knocking on a bit, but there it is! He's got young ideas.
Marjorie But this is wonderful!
Tommy Eh?
Marjorie Don't you see? Our troubles are over.
Tommy Are they?
Marjorie Yes! From now on we won't have to make love in secret!
Tommy No, that's true! We can do it in the kitchen!
Marjorie Oh, I'm so happy, I could cry for joy.
Tommy Oh no, don't cry for *her*. Here! I'll tell you what we'll do.

SONG 5

(*This should be a lightly humorous number, possibly followed by a dance*)

Tommy and Marjorie exit after their song. The Squire enters, followed by the Children. They are trailing behind him sobbing bitterly and very noisily

Squire Shut up! *Shut up! SHUT UP!*

The noise diminishes slightly. The Squire glares at them, at a loss to know what to do

It's no good standing there howling! I keep telling you, there's no room for you in my house. You'll have to go back to Amsterdam.

The Children literally fling themselves at him. He almost collapses under the weight as two small girls grab him round the waist. Their howling grows louder

Children Oh Daddy, don't send us home! We'll be good, Daddy! Oh Daddy, don't turn us out into the street! etc.

The Sheriff enters

Sheriff (*feigning surprise*) Oh Squire! I didn't think you started on 'em at that age!
Squire (*trying vainly to extricate himself*) Fool! I'm not making love to 'em. They belong to my *au pair* girl, and I'm sending 'em home.

The Children howl even louder as they cling tighter to him

Get out of it! Go on, hop it!
Sheriff Sending 'em home? How could you be so cruel?

The howling rises to a shriek

Squire *Shut up!*

The Children quieten down a little

Sheriff Poor little kids!
Squire If you're so fond of them why don't *you* take 'em home?
Sheriff Me?

The Children go deathly quiet

Squire Yes you! There's plenty of room at your house.
Sheriff But I can't—I don't ...

The Children rush over to the Sheriff and molest him

Children (*to the Sheriff*) Daddy! Our new Daddy! (*They encircle him, dancing up and down with enthusiasm*) Darling Daddy!
Sheriff (*shaken to the core*) *I* can't have you. What would my wife say?
Squire You should have heard what mine said!
Children We love you, Daddy.
Sheriff (*freeing himself*) Don't be daft. I'm not your Daddy.
Squire And neither am I.
Sheriff And don't ever say such a thing again. Never!
Squire Half a tick! I've got an idea! (*He pauses, and the children turn to him*) I wonder?

The Children begin to tiptoe towards him

(*Keeping a wary eye on them*) Oh no you don't! Faynights!
Small Girl You can't have faynights.

Act I, Scene 1

Squire Why not?
Small Girl Haven't got your fingers crossed.
Squire (*crossing his fingers quickly*) You know Mother Goose?
Sheriff Yes, everybody knows Mother Goose.
Squire That's her cottage, over there. D'you know something? She hasn't paid me any rent for donkeys' years. Now then, if I chuck her out you kids can sleep in the cottage. Right?
Sheriff You'll have your hands full—chucking her out. She won't even answer the door.
Squire Won't she? I'll see to that! (*He rolls up his sleeves*) Here, you kids wait over there. When Mother Goose opens the door— *you rush in*!
Children Yes, Daddy!
Squire And don't keep calling me Daddy!
Children O.K., Daddy!
Squire Blooming kids!
Sheriff You'll need some help if you're serious about this.
Squire Of course I'm serious.

Tommy and Willy enter

Tommy Reporting for duty, Squire.
Squire Just the chap. Tommy, I'm chucking Mother Goose out of her cottage, and I need your help.
Tommy Very good, Squire.
Squire And Willy, I know you're silly, but you also can lend your might.
Willy (*bringing forth a small girl*) Yes, which one would you like?
Squire No, no! Not that kind of mite! Your muscles, fathead!
Willy I never eat 'em, I love cockles, and d'you know what my mum bought me once ... ?
Squire (*shouting*) Shut up thinking about your silly stomach and listen to me. Once the kids are in, we *men* dash in and chuck all her furniture out. Right?
Sheriff
Tommy } Right! { *speaking together*
Willy
Squire Stand by then! Here we go! Hold your breath!

The Squire tiptoes to the cottage door. He knocks on it with a "pom-tiddly-om-pom" rhythm. After a second it is answered from inside also with a "pom-tiddly-om-pom" rhythm. The Squire glares at the others, then knocks on the door again, but with a different rhythm. It is answered immediately with a like rhythm. The Squire loses his temper and yells

Squire Open this door!
Mother Goose (*from inside*) I'm not in!
Willy It's no use losing your temper, she's not in.
Squire Shut up, imbecile! (*To the Sheriff*) I'll change my tactics. Something a little more subtle.

The Squire tiptoes once more to the cottage and bends down so that his mouth is level with the keyhole. He now addresses Mother Goose in a pleasant "sing-song" style of voice

Mother Goo-hoo-hoose!
Mother Goose (*replying in the same "sing-song" voice*) Squire Taw-haw-dery!
Squire (*in the same sing-song voice*) I've got a surprise for you!
Mother Goose (*in the same voice*) I've got a bigger one for you!
Squire (*losing his temper*) Come *out*! Or I'll knock your front door in!
Mother Goose Come in, and I'll knock your front teeth out!
Squire (*addressing the others*) It's no good. We'll have to use force. Get a pole!

Tommy and Willy go off and return with a long pole. The four men get in position taking hold of the pole with intent to use it as a ramrod. The Children move to an upstage corner

This needs to be highly organized. Now then, when I count three we rush at the door and break through it. Right?
Sheriff
Tommy } Right! { *speaking together*
Willy

Get set! (*As they start a swaying movement*) One—and two—and *THREE*!

They charge towards the door, which opens just a second before they reach it. They go hurtling through the door one behind the other, and disappear from view. There is a loud crash, off. A second's pause, and Mother Goose strolls through the door. She casually dusts her hands as she smiles to the audience

The Children, who are still huddled in their upstage corner, watching events with marked interest, double-up with laughter

Mother Goose Hallo!

Act I, Scene 1   13

Children Hallo!
Mother Goose Who are you?
Children We're Gretchen's brothers and sisters, and we've got nowhere to live.

They all begin to cry

Mother Goose Nowhere to live?
Children No! The Squire's thrown us out on the streets.

They yell double forte

Mother Goose Oh don't cry. There's plenty of room in my house, you can come and live with me.

The Children cheer

From off, up behind Mother Goose's cottage comes the sound of loud "quacking". The sound is very loud and if possible should be amplified with the aid of a microphone

What's that?

The quacking continues and the stage fills with people, the Choristers and Dancers enter from all sides. Everyone is very excited, all talking at once

Choristers What's that? What's going on? ... What's that quacking noise?, etc.

Jack enters from behind the cottage, followed by Jill

Jack Mother! It's Priscilla!
Mother Goose Priscilla?
Jack Yes, she's laying an egg!
All Oooh!

The quacking suddenly stops, and all goes quiet as everyone waits expectantly. We then hear a loud thud

Mother Goose races upstage and disappears behind the cottage. A second's pause and she returns carrying a large golden egg

Mother Goose Look, look! Priscilla's laid a golden egg!
All Oooh!

The Squire, the Sheriff, Tommy and Willy enter through the cottage door. Marjory and Gretchen enter from the opposite side

Squire A golden egg? I don't believe it.

The Squire tries to examine the egg, but Mother Goose pushes him away

Mother Goose Take your thieving hands off!

The quacking starts again. Everyone stops and listens

Goose (*off*) QUACK! ... QUACK! ... QUACK! ...

There is a pause, and then a tremendous thud

> *Mother Goose hands the egg to Jack and hurriedly exits upstage. She emerges carrying a golden egg about twice the size of the previous one*

There is a scream of delight from everyone

Mother Goose Look! It's Pri ... Pri ... Pri ...
Jack Priscilla!

Mother Goose nods her head

Squire (*overcome*) It's big—big—big ...
Mother Goose Bigger!

Squire nods his head, so do all the others, as the quacking starts again

Goose QUACK! QUACK! QUACK! ...

A long pause, and then an ear-splitting thud

Willy Oh dear! I hope she hasn't hurt herself.

Mother Goose hands the egg to Jack who passes hers to Jill. She then runs upstage and staggers back holding a tremendously large golden egg which weighs her down, and Jack and the Sheriff run to her assistance. Everyone is wild with delight

Jack Mother! We're r—r—r ...
Mother Goose Rich!

Jack nods his head

All You're rich! Rich! Hooray!

> *The Goose enters and waddles proudly downstage*

The music strikes up and everyone goes immediately into SONG 6— *a bright biffy chorus*

At the end of the chorus the Lights fade to a BLACK-OUT *and the tabs close*

Act I, Scene 1

A little soft music, which fades out on voice. The stage is in complete darkness. A red spot picks up the Demon who stands L

Demon Ahaah! *(He awaits any audience reaction)*
I am the *Demon*! The man you have to hiss!
But please don't overdo it or a lot of words you'll miss,
Just hiss—and then shut up!
Whenever I come on,
Otherwise the beauty of my diction will be gone.
I appear in every pantomime,
"Gallivanting" like this 'ere,
But my galli's not been vanted
Since approx this time last year.
However, the story this time
Is really not too bad,
It's full of fun and happiness,
My job's to make 'em sad!
This Mother Goose!
She's doing well,
I'll put a stop to that!
I don't like people "doing well",
I like to knock 'em flat.
She's got a goose—so I've been told—
That does a lot of "clucking",
It's laying eggs, I'm told, of gold!
I think this bird wants "plucking!"

He starts to exit

There is a magnesium flash and the Fairy enters R. She stands lit by a white spot.

Fairy *Stay, Demon Cursemall!*
Your wicked threats I heard!
I'll have you know, with magic
I'll protect this lovely bird.
And you won't get away with it,
I'm on the side of "right",
Demon *(to the audience)* Coo! What a blinking stink she's made!
  (to Fairy) You gave me quite a fright!
  (to the audience) I hate that Fairy Tinsel,
  She's always doing that,
  She flashes about like a U.F.O.
  It's worse than paying VAT.

Fairy   And that's just as it should be,
For right doth conquer might.

Demon   Oh, nark it girl,
You're out of date,
Get with it—see the light!

Fairy   And what is so horrendous,
About a story plot,
With people bringing happiness?

Demon   It makes me feel a clot!
Well, take for instance Mother Goose,
She don't need all that "dough",
A woman with a face like hers?
It don't seem apropos!

Fairy   It's apropos that everyone
Shall have a chance in life.
And Mother Goose, like many more,
Has had a life of strife.
For once she's going to be dressed up,
Her wealth is quite unique,
So let us now transport ourselves
To the Gooseyland Boutique!

BLACK-OUT

SCENE 2

Boutique de Gander

An inset scene, i.e. set sufficiently far downstage to enable the back-cloth of the following scene to be hung behind it

A small counter displays various articles of women's lingerie and a fair-sized Union Jack. Standing on the counter is one of the dancers, supposedly a lifeless dummy Model. She wears a leotard and tights and her head is adorned with a large stylish hat. In her right hand she holds a rolled umbrella at the perpendicular. She stands motionless, in an exaggerated pose

Marjorie, the sales girl, and Mother Goose are discovered. Mother Goose is in her underwear, displaying an old-fashioned pair of stays and a pair of long flannel knickers of bright hue. As the scene opens Marjorie is showing Mother Goose a trendy pair of nylon panties

Act I, Scene 2

Marjorie Would Mod*om* care for something like—this?
Mother Goose Oh my goodness! I'd look ravishing in those! Can I try 'em for size?
Marjorie Certainly Mod*om*! Try them for any size you like, and I'll wait outside.

Marjorie exits

Undressing music commences. Mother Goose removes her knickers, displaying a pair of a different colour underneath. She removes those and discloses another pair of yet another hue. She realizes suddenly that the audience are watching and nips behind the counter, where she quickly slips on the modern panties

Squire enters, wearing a tall hat

Music stops. Mother Goose comes to the front of the counter to pick up her loose underwear. She has not seen the Squire's entrance. As she bends to pick up her clothes the Model gives her a sharp slap across the buttocks with the umbrella, then regains her poise. The Squire does not see the Model move. In fact no-one ever sees the business of the Model throughout the entire scene. Mother Goose turns sharply, sees the Squire, and presumes it is him who slapped her. She boxes his ears

Mother Goose You dirty old man!

Mother Goose exits

Squire (*rubbing his face tenderly*) I never did a thing! (*Calling*) Tommy!

Tommy enters

Tommy Is she here, guv'?
Squire Yes, I've just seen her. *And* felt her!
Tommy What's the next move, guv'?
Squire I'm going to butter her up. Buy her some pretty clothes and then try to persuade her to sell me that goose.
Tommy What's she doing now, then?
Squire I'll have a peep through the keyhole and see.

The Squire is about to walk towards the door when the Model gives his hat a clout with her umbrella and knocks it off

(*Turning angrily on Tommy*) Don't do that!
Tommy Do what?

Squire You knocked my hat off.
Tommy I did no such thing.
Squire Well don't do it again.

They argue as Squire puts his hat back on his head

Mother Goose enters, followed by Marjorie

Marjorie You can't stay in here! Mod*o*m is changing.
Squire But I wish to buy Modom Goose a little present.

As he is speaking, Mother Goose turns, apparently to say something to Marjorie, and the Model rubs the handle of her umbrella up and down Mother Goose's back, then quickly regains her poise

Mother Goose (*turning quickly on the Squire*) Oi! Oi! Getting fresh, eh?
Squire I didn't do anything.
Mother Goose You went like "that" up and down my back.
Squire I tell you I *did—not—touch—you*!
Mother Goose Well, someone did. P'raps it was Tommy.
Squire (*turning to Tommy*) Did you go like "that" up and down Mod*o*m Goose's back?

Mother Goose meantime has turned to address Marjorie so that they both have their backs to each other. The Model gives both a sharp smack on the buttocks with the umbrella, then regains her poise. The Squire and Mother Goose turn and face each other, both rubbing their posteriors

Mother Goose } Caught you that time! { *speaking*
Squire *together*
Squire I don't think that's funny.
Mother Goose Then why did you do it?

Tommy turns his back to laugh and the Model gives him a mighty wallop as he bends down

Tommy (*turning on the Squire*) Hi! Cut that out!
Squire Cut what out?
Tommy That hurt!

Tommy gives the Squire a push, and the Squire pushes him back. Tommy gives him a bigger push and he cannons into Mother Goose

Mother Goose (*hopping about on one foot*) Oh! my toe, my toe!
Marjorie (*getting exasperated*) Now! Will you both wait over there please, while I get Mod*o*m measured up?

Act I, Scene 2

The Squire and Tommy go into a corner and sulk, while Marjorie produces a tape measure and goes to Mother Goose

Now Mod*om*, what bust?
Mother Goose Eh?
Marjorie (*raising her voice*) What bust?
Mother Goose I never heard anything.
Marjorie No, no! I mean, what is the size of Mod*om*'s bust?
Mother Goose Oh, I never knew I had one.
Marjorie I will measure Mod*om* ...

She throws her tape measure over Mother Goose's head. The Model catches hold of it with her umbrella, causing it to stretch enormously

(*With furrowed brow, examining the measure*) Good heavens above!
Mother Goose I've been putting on weight lately.
Marjorie You could have fooled me! Now, has Mod*om* any particular colour scheme in mind?
Mother Goose Yes. I don't go much for the little panties. Tell you what, I'll have a nice pair of bloomers made out of that Union Jack—patriotic and healthy!
Marjorie (*drily*) Anything else?
Mother Goose Yes, I'll have that hat. (*She points to the hat on the Model's head*)
Marjorie Which hat?
Mother Goose That one that the model's ...

As Mother Goose faces the Model it bends forward and makes a face at her, putting five fingers up to her nose. Mother Goose screams

Marjorie What is the matter, Mod*om*?
Mother Goose (*excitedly*) That model! It made a face at me!

They all look at the Model, who by now has regained her poise

Marjorie I think Mod*om* is mistaken.
Mother Goose I tell you, I turned round like this, and ...

As she turns to the Model it does it again. Mother Goose gives an earsplitting yell

It did it again!

The Model regains her poise. Everyone stares at her

Marjorie I see nothing strange.
Mother Goose It keeps making faces at me!

Marjorie I think Mod*om*'s had an hallucination.
Squire I think Mod*om*'s had one over the eight.
Mother Goose Listen you! As I faced that Model it bent forward like *this*, and went like *that*!

As Mother Goose bends forward the Model slaps her smartly on the rear. Mother Goose turns to Marjorie

How dare you do that!
Marjorie Do what?
Mother Goose (*repeating her movement*) As I turned to the Squire and bent over like *that*, you went like ...

The Model hits her again

Oooh! You did it again!
Marjorie I did nothing to Mod*om*, Mod*om*!
Mother Goose You clouted Mod*om*'s bott*om*, Mod*om*!
Marjorie I think Mod*om*'s gone bonkers! I'm through!

Marjorie exits

Mother Goose bursts into tears. The Squire puts a protective arm around her

Squire Never mind Mother Goose, don't cry. Listen *I'll* buy you the hat.
Mother Goose (*sobbing bitterly*) You will?
Squire Yes! And any other clothes you want. Come along!

The Squire assists Mother Goose off, then pops his head back and addresses Tommy

Hooray! She's mine, she's mine!

The Squire exits

Tommy You can have her, *I'll* have the Model!

Tommy puts the Model's legs over his shoulders in the manner of a "flying angel" and exits with her

The Lights fade as the tabs close

The Fairy enters, and is lit up by a white spot

Fairy   Poor Mother Goose,
           She's lost her head,
           As folk so often do
           When faced with unexpected wealth,

Act I, Scene 3

No doubt the day she'll rue!
But I must keep an eye on her,
She's clearly on the loose,
I hope she doesn't go too far
Or she will loose her goose!

SONG 7 (*optional*)

At the end of the song the spot fades

SCENE 3

The Wishing Well Glade

This is a typical pastoral scene, with trees and foliage background. A large well is displayed C

The Choristers are grouped around the stage, some sitting on the well

SONG 8

(*It should have a rustic flavour, the Choristers sing it enthusiastically and the Dancers enter and execute a suitable dance*)

They all exit after the number, as Jill enters, followed by Jack

Jack (*breathlessly*) Jill! Jill! What's the hurry? I've been following you everywhere.

Jill I'm sorry, Jack. Or should I address you as Mister, or maybe Sir?

Jack I—I don't get you.

Jill You're a rich man now, you don't wish to keep company with village girls.

Jack Oh Jill, don't be so silly! Wealth has made no difference to me.

Jill Really? Well it has to your mother.

Jack Mother? What has she been doing?

Jill It's what she's *not* been doing.

Jack Meaning?

Jill Speaking—to *me* that is. I'm not good enough for her now.

Jack Jill, darling Jill ...

Jill It's no use Jack. Now that you are rich we can never be anything to each other. Not even friends.

Jill exits

SONG 9

(*It should be a number with a certain amount of pathos, in harmony with the mood*)

At the end of his song Jack exits, and Mother Goose enters. She is now expensively dressed. She swaggers down to the footlights and addresses the audience

Mother Goose Well! How do you like it? It's the latest thing from Oxfam! You remember that pair of knickers they made me out of a Union Jack? D'you know what? First time I wore 'em some fool with a mouth-organ played the National Anthem and the wretched things dropped to half-mast!

The Goose enters. She now wears a pretty little poke bonnet and a cape in matching colours

Oh, doesn't she look pretty? She went to the boutique too, you know!

The Goose executes a large curtsy

(*Aside*) Proper little show-off she is now we're rich. (*In the Goose's ear*) I was just saying you're a proper little show-off.

The Goose affects not to hear, and Mother Goose raises her voice

You've got something to show off about, haven't you?

The Goose nods its head vigorously, and Mother Goose continues to shout into its ear

That lot out there can't lay golden eggs, can they?

The Goose shakes its head

They couldn't even lay a hard-boiled egg, could they?

The Goose jumps up and down in ecstatic glee. Mother Goose opens her purse and takes out a large dummy. She licks it, then pops it into the Goose's mouth. She then takes out a large puff and powders the Goose's nose

The Squire enters

Squire My word, my word! And what a handsome couple you are, to be sure! (*He bends down and examines the Goose more closely*) You know, I hardly recognized you, Mother Goose.

Mother Goose Hi! *I'm* Mother Goose! This one, over here!

Act I, Scene 3   23

Squire Indeed, indeed! I can see the difference quite plainly. I was just examining the Goose's wing span.
Mother Goose So long as you don't want to examine mine!
Squire How much do you want for her?
Mother Goose She's not for sale.

The Goose snuggles up to her

Squire She'd have a good home with me.
Mother Goose She's got a good home with *me*.

The Goose sighs

Squire (*poking the Goose about with his finger*) You are a beautiful bird—beautiful!
Mother Goose (*whose attention has been distracted*) All the boys tell me that.
Squire Not *you* Mother Goose. Good gracious, not *you*! You're no bird, and you're certainly not beautiful.
Mother Goose Really? Don't I remind you of your tainted youth?
Squire No, I'm afraid he died some years ago. I think you *do* remind me of something though. Come to think of it—yes! I once had a very old sheep.
Mother Goose Old sheep!
Squire Yes. It was so old, so old! Its horns were withered up, and its tail was long and lank.

Mother Goose twirls round and round in an effort to find a tail

And yet it was *so* affectionate. Hungry for love! But no-one was hungry enough to fancy it. Poor thing! It was so old you see. So *very* old!

The Squire exits dramatically

Mother Goose Well—let me tell *you* something: there's many a bit of frozen mutton tastes as good as lamb!

Four small Children enter

They cock a snoot as they pass Mother Goose

First Child Oh look! That woman's called Mother Goose.
Second Child H'm! Mutton dressed up as lamb.
Third Child Isn't she ugly?
Fourth Child Yes, I don't know how she can walk about with a face like that.
First Child She's very old.

Second Child You can say *that* again.
Third Child Old and ugly.
All Four Old—and—ugly!

The Children exit, convulsed with laughter

Mother Goose Priscilla! Come here! Now listen carefully. I want you to do something for me. I want you to lay a special egg, an egg that will make me young and beautiful.

The Goose walks away

Will you do it? *Can* you do it?

The Goose drops her head

I thought not! All you can do is lay eggs of gold. Well, I'm fed up with eggs of gold. I want an egg that I can eat, and when I've eaten it I'll be young and beautiful. But you're not clever enough to do that. Get away from me. I hate you! I hate you!

Mother Goose sobs. The Goose sobs

The Demon enters

Demon	Ahaaah! That's right! Hiss me well, For I'm now about to cast a spell. A spell for which I've long been yearning.
Mother Goose	I smell sulphur, Is something burning?
Demon	'Tis me Mother Goose, Look, over here!
Mother Goose	(*seeing him*) Oh my! Oh shucks! Oh crumbs! Oh dear!
Demon	Be not afraid My dear Mother Goose, I'm Demon Cursemall, A man of much use, Tell me your troubles, I'll help if I can.
Mother Goose	Well, you see, I want to be A female Peter Pan!
Demon	To never grow old? And stay beautiful too?
Mother Goose	Yes ... Oh, stop talking in rhyme, You're driving me cuckoo!

Act I, Scene 3

Demon I understand, Mother Goose. And I'll make you a proposition. You shall become young and beautiful on one condition.
Mother Goose What's that?
Demon That you give me Priscilla the Goose!

The Goose runs to Mother Goose and snuggles

Mother Goose Oh no! I could never do that!
Demon (*moving away*) Very well. The deal is off!
Mother Goose No, don't go! Let me consider. How—how would you do it?
Demon In yonder well lies magic water.
Mother Goose Magic water!
Demon Yes. Immerse yourself in it, when you surface you will be young and beautiful.
Mother Goose I can't believe it.
Demon It's true enough. I have put a spell on the water.
Mother Goose How do I know you are speaking the truth?
Demon You must trust me.
Mother Goose (*after reflection*) All right! I'll do it!

Mother Goose goes to the well and looks down. The Goose looks on pathetically

It's no good! I can't do it. I can't leave Priscilla.
Demon The bird has served its purpose. It made you rich, enabled you to buy pretty clothes. But what use are riches and pretty clothes without youth and beauty?
Mother Goose He's right y'know Priscilla. (*She goes to the Goose*) You've been a good little bird. You've made me rich and happy, and I'm grateful. Good-bye Priscilla!

The Goose clings to her

Demon (*getting between them*) Go on bird! Get over there. Come on, scram! Don't worry, I'll make it behave.
Mother Goose Promise you'll be kind to her.
Demon I'll be kind. (*Aside*) All the while she lays eggs of gold!

Mother Goose goes to the well and puts one leg over the side. The Goose runs to her

Mother Goose I can't do it!

Mother Goose walks away from the well with her arm around the Goose

Demon (*losing his cool*) Fool! Idiot! Sentimental numskull! You've had your goose, you've had your gold, now it's your turn to have some fun!
Mother Goose But I *love* her!
Demon To be courted! Admired! Loved!
Mother Goose Loved?
Demon Kissed!
Mother Goose *Kissed!!* Look out well—I'm coming down!

Mother Goose jumps over the side of the well and begins to descend. The Goose exits L. The Choristers enter. They dash on from all sides as they sing the following number, rushing to the well, looking down it, and then running away. In this criss-crossing movement Mother Goose can make her exit unseen by the audience. Alternatively, there can be a brief BLACK-OUT *as she goes over the well*

SONG 10: **Mother Goose is down the well**

Chorus Mother Goose is down the well,
Oh, what a funny tale to tell,
Ha, Ha, Ha, Ha, Ha, Ha, She's
Under such a wicked spell! She's

(*Repeat 8 bars of music*)

Going down, and down, and down,
We hope the lady doesn't drown. She's
Going down, and down, and down,
And down, and down, and down, and down!

(*2nd 8 bars*)

Ha! Ha! Ha! Ha!
Mother Goose is down the well!!
Ha! Ha! Ha! Ha!
Ha, ha, ha, ha, ha, ha, ha!

(*Repeat, and then play to end of strain*)

Ha! Ha! Ha! Ha!
What a funny tale to tell!
Ha! Ha! Ha! Ha!
Ha, ha, ha, ha, ha, ha, ha, ha etc.,

(*continue the laugh till end of strain*)

Act I, Scene 3

The Choristers are left clustered round the well and looking down it. They remain absolutely immobile as the Demon, who throughout the number remains L, speaks

Demon She's down! She's down!
The Goose is mine!
My plan has worked, so all is fine.
She'll take one year to beautify,
Whilst all *Four Seasons* pass her by!
Ha! Ha! Ha!

The Demon exits

Episode *The Four Seasons*

SPRING

As the introductory bars of music strike up the stage comes to life, the Choristers move into positions as they sing

Chorus Merrily the Spring-time brings a song of love,
April showers kiss the flowers,
Early in the morning,
Young man's fancy lightly turns to love sublime,
And everybody's happy in the Spring-time.

They sing a repeat chorus as the Dancers enter, falling backstage to leave room for the dance. After dance, Dancers and Chorus exit

Gretchen and the Squire enter from opposite sides. Their costumes are notably Spring-like

Squire (*falling on his knees*)
You promised to wed me in glorious Spring,
I'll buy the home dear, I'll buy the ring.
Just name the day dear, Say you'll be mine,
Spring-time is ring-time, Spring-time divine.

Gretchen (*walking away*)
A wedding in Spring?
T'would be such a crime,
A season with any reason or rhyme,
The weather's uncertain,
Might rain all the time,
Se we'll marry ...

Squire (*rising, hopefully*) Marry?
Gretchen Yes! We'll marry in Summer time!

The Squire and Gretchen exit on opposite sides as the introduction for the next number strikes up, and Willy, Sheriff, and Choristers enter

SUMMER

All	The Summer is coming, Hurrah! Hurrah! On holiday packages we'll go far,
Willy **Sheriff** }	To Spain and Marjorca, To Gozo and Malta, And Rome and Gibralta, And Shangri-la!
All	The sun will shine in the sky, Tra-la! And rain will definitely say, Ta-ta! We'll drink as we dream, And we'll munch our ice-cream, For Summer is coming, Hurrah! Hurrah

Reprise Chorus Tutti (*with a fair amount of robust movement*)

   All exit as the Dancers enter

The dance should be boisterous and happy

   The Dancers exit. Gretchen and the Squire enter, in summer attire

Squire You promised to wed me in Summer sublime,
The season for marriage, with reason and rhyme,
Just name the day dear, Say you'll be mine,
Summer time, Ring time, Summer sublime!

Gretchen A marriage in Summer is foolish I fear,
Impossible season, the worst of the year,
The sky's overcast, and thunder I hear!

Thunder is heard

   So we'll marry ...

Squire Marry?

Gretchen We'll marry when Autumn is here!

The Squire and Gretchen exit at opposite sides as Willy, Sheriff, and the Choristers enter

Act I, Scene 3

AUTUMN

All Now the Autumn comes, With its sky so grey,
And the leaves all fall, At the break of day,
D'ye ken John Peel as his horses neigh?
'Tis his hounds and his horn in the morning.

Willy But it's nice and snug,
Sheriff In our cosy bed,
And it's cold outside,
Makes your head like lead,
So you couldn't care less,
For you feel half dead,
As the chill makes you ill in the Autumn!

Reprise

All As you whirl and wheel, And ye ken John Peel,
For the hunt's begun, And you shout and squeal,
'Ere the days draw in, And the fogs begin,
For we're fastly approaching the Autumn.

Willy He can keep his hunt,
Sheriff Can dear old John,
With his dogs and his horse
Which he sits upon,
Draw the blinds—stoke the fire!
Put the telly on,
'Cos it's warmer inside in the Autumn!

All exit as the last four bars are repeated

All Draw the blinds—stoke the fire!
Put the telly on,
'Cos it's warmer inside in the Autumn!

*The Dancers enter, execute a vigorous "Pony Trot", and exit.
Gretchen and the Squire enter in suitable costume*

Squire You promised to wed me when Autumn was here,
The season best suited! You said it my dear,
"Honeymoon time," The best of the year,
Shall wedding bells ring, the parson appear?

Gretchen A wedding in Autumn, is quite out of date,
Not "with-it" luv, t'would be trifling with fate,
And what could be worse than our Autumn clime?
So we'll marry ...

Squire	Marry?
Gretchen	We'll marry in Winter Time!

Gretchen and the Squire exit on opposite sides

Willy, the Sheriff and the Choristers enter

WINTER

All	Now we come to Winter, It's the season steeped in rhyme,
Willy **Sheriff**	We take our snuff and sniff it up,
All	For the sake of Auld Lang Syne!
Willy **Sheriff**	With turkeys stuffed, and Christmas pud', We'll sniff our snuff and stuff,
All	Cold Winter's here, But lots of cheer, For it's nearly Christmas time.

Reprise with marked acceleration

> So take a cup and drink it up,
> The stuff that tastes like wine,
> Do *not* gyrate—just hibernate,
> In the good old Winter Time.

Reprise again, as all dance off still singing

The Dancers enter, do an applicable dance and exit

Gretchen and the Squire enter, in overcoats and scarves

Gretchen (*brightly*)	Cold Winter has come, I will now name the day, Yours now for ever, For ever and aye! A wedding of snows is the one that I choose, You ask for my hand? I no longer refuse!
Squire (*turning away*)	I cannot alas, ask you to say "Yes", I'm false and I'm faithless, That I confess, You wouldn't decide, The word would not speak, So I married ...

Act I, Scene 3   31

Gretchen Married?

Squire I married!

Gretchen
(*shrieking*) He's married ...

Squire I married your Aunty last week!

A severe-looking Woman enters at speed. Two or three scruffy Kids cling to her skirts

She grabs the Squire's arm and pulls him away. The Kids dance round him

Kids Daddy! Our new Daddy! Darling Daddy! etc.

The Lights fade to a BLACK-OUT

During the short BLACK-OUT *Mother Goose enters, unseen by the audience, and takes her place inside the well*

When the Lights come up the stage is empty

Then Mother Goose appears—first her head, and after a short pause the rest of her. She steps out of the well and minces round the stage. She is made up to look pretty, with a youthful wig and trendy clothes. She eventually swaggers down-stage and addresses the audience

Mother Goose Bet you didn't know who I was! Did you? I bet none of 'em recognize me! Wanna bet? (*She looks off*) Look out! Somebody coming. Don't let on who I am, will you?

Tommy and Marjorie enter. They pass Mother Goose. Tommy then pauses and looks back

Tommy (*to Marjorie*) I say! My word! What a very pretty girl.
Mother Goose (*aside*) I *told* you!
Marjorie Where?
Tommy Back there!
Marjorie Oh yes, charming.
Tommy I wonder if she can help us?
Marjorie Well don't be shy, ask her.
Tommy (*to Mother Goose*) Excuse me, fair maid.
Mother Goose (*in a very affected voice*) Oh, young man. How you startled me!
Tommy I'm so sorry.

Mother Goose What would you be a-wanting?
Tommy We are looking for a goose.
Mother Goose A goose?
Marjorie Yes, we understand one has been seen wandering this way.
Tommy And the Squire is offering a lot of money for it.
Mother Goose He'll be lucky!
Tommy It lays golden eggs.
Mother Goose I know!
Tommy What?
Mother Goose I mean—I know of no such goose.
Marjorie It belongs to an ugly old woman called Mother Goose!
Mother Goose Mother Goose?
Marjorie D'you know her?
Mother Goose Never heard of her!
Tommy You can't miss her, she has an ugly-looking growth behind her nose!
Mother Goose (*slightly shattered*) When did she get *that*, I wonder?
Tommy I don't know when she got it, but she calls it her face!

Tommy and Marjorie exit laughing

Mother Goose I told you they wouldn't recognize me.

SONG 11

Mother Goose exits after her number. Jill enters, followed by Jack

Jack Jill! Jill! Have you heard the news? We're poor again.
Jill Oh Jack! Is this true?
Jack Yes! Mother has sold Priscilla.
Jill But, but Priscilla should be worth a fortune!
Jack Mother sold her for a course of Beauty Treatment!
Jill Oh no! The Devil must have got into her!
Jack He did!
Jill Oh Jack! I'm so sorry.
Jack Well I'm not! Now that I'm just a poor lad again, maybe I can—maybe *we* can ...
Jill I think I know what you mean.

SONG 12

The number commences as a duet

  The Choristers and Dancers quickly enter and join in

Act I, Scene 3

Towards the end, or if preferred on a reprise, the music comes to a sudden stop. Everybody looks upwards, and points

All Look! Look! What's that?
A Voice (*shouting excitedly*) Looks like an airship!
Another Voice It's an aeroplane!
Another Voice It's a helicopter!
Another Voice It's a flying saucer!

All eyes travel from L to R as they watch the path of the flying object

All Principals, except the Demon and the Fairy, enter

Mother Goose (*shouting above the din*) It's Priscilla! My Goose! It's Priscilla!

There is a magnesium flash

The Fairy enters R and the Demon enters L

Demon The goose has escaped! My plan is unstuck!
 My goose with gold eggs, Has become a Dead Duck!
Fairy Yes, Demon Cursemall, Your plan is dead flat,
 The goose has escaped! I saw to that!
 She has flown away, Where you'll never get her,
 to The Mountains of Snow!
Demon Is that so?
(*with* Well you'd better
sarcasm) Get cracking with the magic you know,
 'Cos I'll follow that goose
 To the Mountains of Snow,
 And I'll bring her back, you see if I won't,
Fairy I'll use ev'ry trick to see that you don't!

The Demon exits, snarling

The Fairy turns and addresses the crowd

Fear not! I'll guard Priscilla on her perilous flight. She has gone to seek justice from the King of Gooseland. He lives the other side of the Snow Mountains. You must hurry there or you will lose her, for the Court of Justice will take her away from you for ever if they find you guilty of neglecting her. So hurry! Hurry to the Mountains of Snow!

All (*with raised voices*) To the Mountains of Snow!

They sing the last phrase of the Production Number, the singing and music rising to a crescendo as they form a tableau and—

the CURTAIN *falls*

ACT II

Scene 1

The Snow Mountains

In the distance can be seen the snow-clad mountains. Peeping just above them is the upper part of Gooseland Palace which appears to nestle somewhere in between them. It has the appearance of a Fairy Castle

Snowman Mime

The Lighting is predominantly blue. A property-built snowman stands C. The Dancers are miming the completion of the snowman, patting and stroking him. One enters with an eye, she pirouettes across stage and sticks the eye in the appropriate place. Another enters with the other eye. She is followed immediately with others carrying his nose and mouth. Then other dancers enter, each carrying a large pom-pom which they adjust down his front. Lastly, one enters carrying his old top hat which she perches on his head. They continue to dance round the snowman during and after the mime. Meantime the Choristers are grouped about the stage singing an appropriate song.

SONG 13

At the end of the Mime and song the Dancers and Choristers exit. Some Children enter dragging a sledge (optional) on which is seated Father Christmas. He carries a pack on his back. He rises, and the Children exit, dragging the sledge and the snowman off with them

Father Christmas (*walking downstage and addressing the audience*) I've got lots of nice little gifts here in my sack. I wonder who they're for? Let's see! (*He fishes in his sack and withdraws a small packet which he pretends to read*) For the nice little girl in the third row with long fair hair. (*He throws the packet out to someone in the third row, then brings forth another. He varies his patter according to requirements, throwing out as*

Act II, Scene 1

many gifts as desirable. The little packages can contain sweets, small toys, fruit, or anything else suitable)

Father Christmas exits, as the Sheriff and Willy enter. They each have a basket of property snowballs. They enter from opposite sides and immediately commence pelting each other with the prop snowballs. Then Willy suddenly stops

Willy Here, let's have a game of snowballs with the boys and girls out there.

Sheriff Good idea! (*He addresses the audience*) Anyone like to play snowballs? Right! We'll throw 'em at *you* and you throw them back at *us*!

They then throw their snowballs at the audience. When this has gone far enough they go into a comedy duet

SONG 14

This has a rollicking chorus in which the audience can take part

At the end of the song Willy and the Sheriff exit. Tommy and Marjorie enter, they are holding hands and look a little weary. They walk across the stage as they talk

Tommy Well, we're getting nearer. We're half-way up the Snow Mountains.

Marjorie Are you sure Priscilla will be there?

Tommy Oh yes, that's where the Fairy said she was making for. Gooseland Palace is just the other side.

Marjorie Safely tucked away, where no-one can harm them.

Tommy Yes. Funny how people can be cruel to geese. They're such lovely things I always think.

Marjorie Me too.

Tommy Come on, there's a nice little cove up there, we'll take a little break and then continue on our way.

SONG 15

Tommy and Marjorie exit after their duet. The Squire enters. He is puffing and blowing

Squire By! What a climb! I don't know if that darned goose is worth it. Even if I find her I don't suppose I'll catch her. Even if I catch her I shan't know what to do with her; provided I can get her home to *do* it; that it!

Mother Goose enters. She is still in her youthful make-up

(*doing a double-take when he sees her*) By heck! What a smasher! Er, Madam! Lady! Er, Missis! You—you—you—*are beautiful!*
Mother Goose (*coyly*) I know I am!
Squire Come to me! Come—and fan my ardour
Mother Goose I wouldn't denigrate my fan.
Squire Alas, alack! I have been smitten!
Mother Goose Not as yet, but you soon will be.
Squire Smitten by your beauty. It is driving me insane.
Mother Goose You didn't have far to go.
Squire Your eyes, your cheeks, your noses!
Mother Goose Noses? I've only got one!
Squire I can see two from here.
Mother Goose You must have had a couple.
Squire And your lips! They are like two roses.
Mother Goose What kind of roses?
Squire Two roses of houses. Come! Be my little honey bee!

Mother Goose hops round the stage, waving her arms up and down and buzzing like a bee

What is your name, my pretty?
Mother Goose Gerty Bubblegum.
Squire How do you spell it?
Mother Goose You don't spell it, you chew it.
Squire Oh Gerty, don't be flirty! (*He throws his arms around her*)
Mother Goose (*disentangling herself*) Oh Percy, have a bit of mercy!
Squire Gerty Bubbleygum! Come, rest your head upon my manly bosom!
Mother Goose Oh swain! (*She nestles*)
Squire Beg your pardon?
Mother Goose Swain.
Squire Sorry!
Mother Goose Dost thou love me, swain?
Squire I certainly dost.
Mother Goose Then we're a couple of dusters!

SONG 16

This should be a burlesque love duet, and if possible finish with an eccentric dance

Mother Goose and the Squire exit after the duet

Act II, Scene 1

The Lights dim and soft music is heard

The Goose enters. She is obviously exhausted

She limps C and looks around her. She looks this way and that, shakes herself, and attempts to fly. The effort is too much, and she drops her head, then sinks to the floor

Gretchen enters

Gretchen Why, it—it's Priscilla! (*She runs to the Goose, kneels by her side, and puts a protecting arm around her*) You poor little soul! You're absolutely exhausted, you must have been flying for hours. Look at you! Poor little soul! (*She helps the Goose up*) Everybody's searching for you. Have you seen Mother Goose?

The Goose shakes its head sadly, and begins to cry

She wants you back! She *does* Priscilla! She's searching for you madly, she went on ahead of me. She's sorry for what she did. She wants you to forgive her.

The Goose walks away. Gretchen follows her as once more she sinks to the ground

Oh dear! You poor old thing! Can't you fly at all?

The Goose shakes her head

(*In despair*) Oh dear, what can I do? Try to raise up a little. That's better. (*She helps the Goose up*) Splendid! Now flap your wings. Go on! Keep trying! Flap—flap—flap!

The Goose moves her wings but eventually drops back exhausted

Oh dear! I'll have to get help! Tell you what Priscilla, you rest here a little while, I'll go farther up the mountain and find the others. Not to worry now! I'll be back in a jiffy!

Gretchen exits R

The music stops and there is a cymbal crash

The Demon enters L. He is picked up by a red spot

Demon Ahaaaah!
So there you are, my pretty goose!
You've had a few days on the "loose".
But you will not escape again,
Just slip your neck inside this noose!

From under his cape he produces a short length of rope which is looped at one end. He places the loop over the Goose's neck and begins to drag her off

>Now! Take it easy, that's a good girl!
>Get not your feathers out of curl!
>Aaah! Aaah! Steady! *This* way, please!
>I'll get you home by slow degrees.

The Goose continues to resist, and the Demon loses his temper

>Come on! Curse you!—Not so slow!

He kicks the Goose

>Take *that*! And *that*!
>Now will you go?
>Go on—that's better,
>You're now doing fine. (*He gets the Goose moving*)
>Ahaaah! Once more the goose is mine!

The Demon drags the Goose off L. The Fairy enters R

Fairy The goose is yours! But not for long,
I'll keep watch, and right this wrong,
All men shall seek, till she is found,
To save her we're in honour bound.

The Fairy exits R. Gretchen enters R

Gretchen Priscilla! Priscilla! Where are you? (*She looks around*) She's gone! Ah, bless her! She must have regained her strength and taken to the air again. What a good job, I couldn't see hair or hide of the others. Still, so long as Priscilla is safe that's all that matters. Oh, I'm so happy!

SONG 17

Gretchen exits after her number. Jack and Jill enter

Jill Oh Jack, I can't go any farther!
Jack We'll have to settle down for the night and continue our search in the morning.
Jill They say these mountains are haunted.
Jack I don't believe in ghosts.
Jill Well—I don't know.
Jack Nervous?

Jill Not when I'm with you.

Mother Goose enters

Mother Goose Ah, there you are, my son. Where have you been and who is that girl you're bothering with?
Jack Oh, Mother, I'm courting.
Mother Goose Courting?
Jack Yes, I'm in love.
Mother Goose In love? A boy your age?
Jack Mother, I'm grown up! I want to get married.
Mother Goose Married? You come to your Mother for advice if you want to get married. A woman who's been through it from A to Z, and *she* will tell you to look before you leap.
Jack Mother! Did Father look before he leapt?
Mother Goose Not likely, I leapt before he had time to look.
Jill Have you seen anything of Priscilla, Mother Goose?
Mother Goose No, and it's getting dark, and there's a lot of strange men about. I shall have to bed down for the night.
Jill Oh, do be careful. They say these hills are haunted.
Mother Goose Then I'm going straight back home to get my nightgown.
Jill Your nightgown?
Mother Goose Yes. I'm not having any ghost watching me sleeping without my nightgown on.

Mother Goose exits

SONG 18

Jack and Jill exit after their song. The Dancers enter for a "Skeleton Dance" (optional). They exit after the dance is over

Mysterioso music commences. The Lights dim

Mother Goose enters, followed by the Squire, the Sheriff and Willy. Each is attired in a very eccentric nightgown, and an old-fashioned nightcap. They walk on one behind the other, led by Mother Goose who is carrying a lighted candle

They take large stealthy steps in time with the orchestra who play a few weird chords in slow tempo. When they stop walking the music stops. They pause, look back, then do three small quick steps. The music keeps in perfect rhythm. They pause again, then take two very long slow steps. The music complies. Eventually the music stops

Squire (*in a hoarse whisper*) I'm not nervous!
Willy Neither am I.
Mother Goose Then what are you shivering for?
Willy It's the wind blowing up my nighty!
Sheriff Let's sleep over here.

They go up C

Mother Goose Let's all huddle together, nice and close.

Mother Goose places the lighted candle on the floor and they all make a dash and lie down

Well, good night boys!

Squire
Sheriff } Good night, Mother Goose. { *speaking together*
Willy

A Loud Voice (*off, through microphone*) GOOD NIGHT!

All four start up and look at each other

Mother Goose (*to Squire*) Was that you?
Squire No, I thought it was you.
Mother Goose Did *you* do that Willy?
Willy No, I was fast asleep, dreaming.
Sheriff You always are.
Mother Goose Well, *someone* said "Goodnight", and it wasn't us.
Willy P'raps it was one of the mountain goats.
Squire Silly goat!
Sheriff Well, let's lie down and get some sleep.

They lie back, then the Squire sits up again

Squire Just a minute. Who's going to blow the candle out?
Mother Goose (*sitting up*) Good question.
Willy You brought it in, you blow it out.

Mother Goose hies herself up reluctantly

Mother Goose I don't know how you men would get along without we women. Please do this, please do that, now it's blow the candle out. It's fair sickening. (*She opens her mouth, takes in an enormous intake of breath and blows. But her mouth slips round to the left side of her face, so that she is unable to blow straight at the flame*) Oh dear! I'm bewitched! Look!
Sheriff (*sitting up*) What's the matter?
Mother Goose I can't blow the candle out!

Act II, Scene 1

Sheriff Can't blow the candle out? What nonsense! (*He rises and snatches the candle out of her hand irritably*) Women! You're all the same! Incompetent!

Mother Goose Well, you blow it out then.

Sheriff I will. Watch me! (*He takes a big breath and blows. But his mouth slithers round to the right side of his face. He blows and blows, without success. Talking out from the right side of his mouth*) Oh dear! Look what's happened to me!

Mother Goose Now *you're* bewitched. Goody-goody!

Willy (*getting up and coming down stage*) Here, what's going on? Why don't you blow the candle out and let us get some sleep?

Sheriff (*handing the candle to Willy*) Well you blow it out then.

Willy takes a huge breath and blows hard, but his lower lip suddenly protrudes so that he can only blow upwards towards his nose

Willy Oh dear, or lor', oh gracious me! Now I'm bewitched!

The Squire jumps up and comes down stage

Squire Too much telly, that's your trouble.
Willy I can't blow the candle out.
Sheriff I can't blow the candle out.
Mother Goose I can't blow the candle out.
Squire Can't blow the candle out? I never heard such drivel! Give the candle to me. (*He takes the candle with a pompous gesture and gives an enormous blow. But his upper lip protrudes, so that he is blowing downwards towards his chest*)

The others gather round him in alarm

Others Keep trying, keep trying.

The Squire blows till he is red in the face, but without avail. The others join in and blow too

A small Girl enters, dressed in a pretty little nightgown

Small Girl Hey! What's going on here?
Squire I can't blow the candle out!
Willy I can't blow the candle out!
Sheriff I can't blow the candle out!
Mother Goose I can't blow the candle out!

Each shouts the above line with his mouth in the deformed position

Small Girl (*nonchalantly*) Give it here! (*She grabs the candlestick with her left hand, licks the first finger and thumb of her right hand, snuffs the candle out and hands it back*) There y'are!
Mother Goose Well I'm blowed!
Small Girl Yes, but you didn't blow straight, did you?

The small Girl exits

The mouths of the others revert to their normal shapes

Squire Well! Now perhaps we can *all* get some sleep.
Mother Goose Shhh! Don't shout so loud, you'll wake the ghosts.
Sheriff Oh, *do* stop talking about ghosts!

They all settle down up C and lie down. Mysterioso music

Willy (*rising after a few seconds*) I can't sleep without a nightlight. Anyone got a match?
Mother Goose What are you going to do?
Willy Light the candle.

A man in period dress enters. He carries his head under his arm. He is lit by a green spot

The Man walks C with slow deliberate steps, stops, and faces front. Willy meantime discusses with the others in mime the desirability of a lighted match. None has seen the ghost. Willy rises and comes down stage holding the candle in his hand. The others lie back and feign sleep

(*Addressing the audience*) Anyone got a match? A match—to light the candle ... (*He sees the man for the first time, and walks towards him*) 'Scuse me mate. Got a match on you?

The Man turns and faces him: Willy gives a shriek, jumps in the air, races round the stage and exits, followed by the Man

There is a short pause. Then Mother Goose sits up and looks round

Mother Goose What's happened to Willy?
Squire (*sitting up*) Eh?
Mother Goose Willy? Where's he gone?
Squire (*settling down again*) How should I know?
Mother Goose He was here a minute ago.
Sheriff (*sitting up*) P'raps he's gone to see a man about a mountain goat. (*He laughs uproariously at his own joke*)
Mother Goose Very funny! (*She calls*) Willy! Willy! Where are you?

Act II, Scene 1

Mother Goose gets up and goes to look off. She calls his name and then turns to the others

No sign of him that way ...

As Mother Goose speaks, a hand attached to a long pole comes through the aperture and pokes her on the buttocks. Mother Goose gives a scream and rushes back to the others. They all jump up, asking her "What's the matter", etc

Mother Goose (*trying to get her breath*) A great big hand—it came out of the ether—and, and clouted me on my auroraborealis!
Others Where?
Mother Goose Over there!

The other three go to the side of the stage and furtively look off. Mother Goose, thoroughly shattered, retreats backwards towards the opposite exit

Squire I can't see anything.
Sheriff There's nothing out here.
Squire Perhaps you dreamt it.

Meantime, another hand, similarly attached to a pole, comes through and strikes her posterior. She gives a scream and rushes to the others

Mother Goose It did it again! Over there this time!

The others run to the opposite side, leaving Mother Goose, who turns her back on the exit as she watches them. They both look off, then turn to Mother Goose. As they do so, the hand comes through and gives them both a dig in the rear. Simultaneously the other hand comes through Mother Goose's side and touches her. They all yell and rush C, where they lie down, hiding their heads.

A very tall Ghost enters

The Ghost walks slowly round the stage. After a few seconds the four sit bolt upright, give a yell and begin to run this way and that, crisscrossing and stumbling into each other

They all eventually exit, with the Ghost in hot pursuit

The Lights fade to a BLACK-OUT *as the tabs close.*

Scene 2

The stage is dark. There is a little soft music

The Demon enters R. He is dragging the Goose by her rope. They are picked up by a red spot. They cross L

Demon Ahaaah! Ahaaah!
We are safely on our way,
Come, Goosey darling, don't delay.
And struggle not—you're firmly hooked,
Ahaaah! My goose will soon be cooked!

The Demon drags the Goose off L. The Fairy enters R. She is picked up by a white spot.

Fairy You've said it, Demon Cursemall!
And please don't think I'm being personal,
Your goose *is* cooked! So hark me well,
I'm now about to cast a spell!

She makes a big flourish with her wand

I evoke the powers of Fairyland,
To put their strength at my command,
And *FREE PRISCILLA*! (*She waves her wand*)
RIGHT AWAY! (*She waves again*)
She's gone!
She's free!
She comes this way!

She looks up and points, as though seeing the Goose flying from L to R. The Lights come up to full. The music rises to crescendo, then dies down as she speaks

On broken wing she flies supreme,
She's up there in the air,
The King of Gooseland waits for her,
Within his Palace fair.
See, there she goes, the plucky Goose,
Now firmly on her way,
So let us all give her a cheer,
Hooray! Hooray! Come on, *HOORAY!*

The Fairy exits R

The music fades out

Act II, Scene 2

The Squire enters L, followed by Gretchen

Squire Come on, come on! What a slow coach you are. The others must have reached the Palace long ago.

Gretchen (*breathlessly*) Listen! I came to you as an *au pair* girl, not an alpine climber-upper!

Squire You don't understand. If Mother Goose gets there before me I shall have to divorce my wife and marry her.

Gretchen Marry Mother Goose, what for?

Squire (*mysteriously*) It's the only way I'll get possession of the Goose!

Gretchen You don't want the Goose—you're not such a silly goose. *You* want the golden eggs that are *laid* by the Goose.

Squire I'm getting goose-flesh listening to you. You leave me speechless.

Gretchen You know what they say? When you're stuck for words, say it in song.

SONG 19

Gretchen and the Squire exit after their number. Mother Goose enters, and, from the opposite side, the Sheriff and Willy

Sheriff Ah, there you are Mother Goose. We've been looking for you.

Mother Goose I was held up by one of the guards. He wanted to frisk me!

Willy Oh I say!

Mother Goose He threatened to frisk me all over to see if I had any money.

Sheriff Whatever did you do?

Mother Goose I said "Well, I haven't any money, but if you frisk me all over I'll give you a post-dated cheque."

Sheriff So he let you go free!

Mother Goose Yes, however did you guess?

Sheriff *We've* been to Gooseland Palace. Right inside the Court of Justice.

Mother Goose You have?

Willy Yes, the guards arrested us and took us prisoners.

Mother Goose Prisoners?

Willy Fortunately we escaped.

Sheriff But all the others are there. The King of Gooseland's got the lot. He's in a terrible temper.

Mother Goose Why, what happened?
Sheriff We all trooped into the Palace, large as life, looking for Priscilla. And the King's Guards pounced on us.
Willy Oh they are a funny lot. They're made of wood.
Mother Goose Made of wood?
Willy Yes, they walk like this! And turn round like this!
Sheriff They're just like wooden soldiers you'd buy in a shop.
Willy How they can live with a wooden head I don't know!
Mother Goose Well you've managed it for a few years.
Sheriff Your son Jack's there, and Jill.
Willy And the King's waiting for *you*. He holds you responsible.
Mother Goose Responsible for what?
Willy The way you treated Priscilla.
Sheriff And when he gets you he's going to kill you.
Mother Goose If he does I'll never speak to him again.
Sheriff They're all waiting now for Priscilla. As soon as she turns up the trial will begin.
Willy Meantime, they're singing songs to keep the King amused before he cuts their heads off.
Mother Goose It's a good idea.
Willy What is?
Mother Goose To sing 'em *before* he cuts their heads off. And I've got another idea. Let *us* learn a song to sing to him, and let's make it so charming, so alluring, that he'll give stay of execution till further notice.
Sheriff Probably hurry it up all the more.
Mother Goose Now, what shall we sing?
Sheriff Something we know.
Willy Something we all know.
Mother Goose I've got it. This one ...

SONG 20

(*A popular chorus in which the audience are invited to join, with possibly the words of the song written up on a "Song Sheet"*)

SCENE 2

The Royal Court of Justice

It is an ornate colourful scene, with a central staircase leading up to a high rostrum.

Act II, Scene 2

Seated on a golden throne at the apex of the staircase is the King of Gooseland.

He is surrounded by a bodyguard of Wooden Soldiers (the Dancers) and inside the circle are a small flock of geese (the Children).

Practically all the Principals are on with the Choristers. They are grouped in front of the King as they entertain him with a song—preferably a well-harmonized number

SONG 21

King Thank you. You sing very well—for mortals!
Jack Thank you, Your Majesty.
King (*almost reluctantly*) Never-the-less, it is my duty to try you for the loss of one of Gooseland's most treasured birds.
Jack Your Majesty! I'm sure Priscilla is not lost.
King Then where is she? And where is your mother?
Jack Mother will be here soon, and so will Priscilla.
King Why did your mother do this thing?
Jack As I've already explained, Your Majesty. Mother wouldn't harm Priscilla, it was just a silly whim. She wanted youth and beauty.
King So, she sold the Goose to the Devil!
Jack Yes, I mean No! Your Majesty, my mother *loved* Priscilla. She is a *good* woman.
King Then why does she not come?
Jack She is on her way, searching all the time for her beloved Goose.
King (*shouting*) *My* beloved Goose! She has proved unworthy of owning such a bird.

Mother Goose bursts into the room, followed by Willy and the Sheriff

Mother Goose Jack! I've found you at last.
Jack Mother!
Mother Goose I've been looking for you everywhere. Where have you been, how did you get here before me, what is this place, and who is that horrid-looking creature sitting up-top of them stairs?
Jack Hush, Mother! He's the King.
Mother Goose King Kong?
Jack No, the King of Gooseland!

Mother Goose (*all confused*) Oh, the King of Goose—the Goose of King ... (*She goes towards the King and executes an enormous curtsy*) The King of Gooseland! Your very royal Gandership! I've heard so much about you.

King You, I presume, are Mother Goose?

Mother Goose Oh, your Gander! Your presumption was never more in evidence.

King *Seize her!*

Two Guards come down and stand either side of Mother Goose. Their movements are stiff and jerky, as though made of wood. They grab her arms

Mother Goose Here! Be careful of your splinters!

King The bird, madam, you call Priscilla has, it seems, disappeared.

Mother Goose Well, your Gandership, it was just a bit of devilry with the Devil. No harm meant!

King *Silence!*

Mother Goose Well, don't shout, I'm not blind.

King You shall share the fate meted out to all mortals guilty of cruelty to geese. (*He rises and comes down the stairs*) D'you follow me?

Mother Goose (*falling in behind him*) Certainly, where are we going?

King *Hold her!*

The two Guards pull her back

Mother Goose (*pushing them away and rubbing her arms*) Oh! those splinters again!

King (*in solemn tones*) I now pronounce sentence according to the laws of Gooseland. I find you guilty of abandoning a goose named Priscilla and in consequence you shall suffer death in the manner suffered by geese by mortals. Do you understand, madam?

Mother Goose (*bobbing and scraping*) Oh yes, your very reverent goosegog, I know exactly what you mean, but I don't know what you're talking about.

King In the same way that people kill and eat geese so will we execute *you!*

Mother Goose Oh yes, I think I'm beginning to get the picture.

King First—your neck shall be *rung!*

Mother Goose (*making a choking noise*) Rung?

Act II, Scene 2

King Yes, rung!
Mother Goose It's not a *bell*!
King Then—you shall be *stuffed*!
Mother Goose Well, I've oft been told to get ...
King (*shouting*) *STUFFED*!
Mother Goose That's right!
King Then—you shall be basted in boiling oil!
Mother Goose I've oft been in hot water, but ...
King Then ...
Mother Goose Now for the good news!
King You shall frizzle! Frizzle on the end of a sharp hook!
Mother Goose Could I not have just a wee turn on the spit?
King (*losing his temper*) Silence! Gabbling woman! Prepare to meet your fate. (*To the Guards*) Stoke the fires!
Guards (*calling off*) Stoke the fires!
King Prepare the meal!
Guards Prepare the meal!

There is general consternation

The Goose enters during it, and moves C

A dramatic pause

King My Goose!
Mother Goose *My* Goose!

There is a cymbal crash and a magnesium flash

The Demon enters L

Demon *My* Goose!

The Demon makes a huge gesture and everyone remains perfectly still as though mesmerized

Ahaaah! The Goose is *mine*! (*He struts towards Priscilla and is about to grab her*)

The Fairy enters R

The Lights dim, leaving the Fairy and the Demon lit respectively by a white and a red spot

Fairy Stay, Demon Cursemall!
You've played your game and lost!

She waves her wand over the Goose

Wickedness will never pay,
As you've found to your cost.

The Demon begins to wilt

Demon My strength is ebbing fast,
Oh, help me someone do!
I'm on my knees,
I'm on my tum,
I can't believe it's true!

Fairy It's true enough—you monster!
You ought to be ashamed.

Demon (*grovelling on the ground*)
I'm *sorry* folk!
I really am,
(*aside*) By jove, I *have* been tamed!

Fairy Then go!
And seek your sanctuary
Within your own Nirvana.

Demon (*crawling off on his stomach*)
I go! I go!
My head is low,
I feel a proper nana!

The Demon exits

Fairy Our story's nearly ended,
But hearts yet to be won,
So carry on dear mortals,
This lapse in time is done!

The Fairy exits

As she does so, the Lights return to full, and everyone resumes movement

King One moment! The fate of this goose shall be decided by a very simple expedient. (*To Mother Goose*) You say she loves *you*. I think her wish is to remain with *me*. We will spread ourselves away from her and let her choose.

The King takes a few paces R of the Goose and Mother Goose goes L

Come Priscilla! Make your choice! Who do you want?

Act II, Scene 2   51

The Squire meantime comes down stage and tries to attract the Goose's attention

Squire (*in stage whisper*) Priscilla! Priscilla! Come to Uncle Tawdry!

There is a dramatic pause while the Goose makes up her mind, going from the King to Mother Goose, ignoring the Squire, then eventually rushing to Mother Goose, who throws her arms around her

Mother Goose Priscilla darling! Come to Mother!
Jack You see your majesty, the Goose *loves* my mother.
King I am well satisfied.
Mother Goose (*to Priscilla*) Oh you do look so dishevelled, I should think old Nick's been using your feathers for pipe cleaners.
Jack And are we now forgiven, Your Majesty, and may we please go?
King The first answer to your question is "yes". But why in such a hurry to go? I'm beginning to like you.
Jack It's rather personal, It's Jill ...
Jill I have just consented to be his wife.
All Hooray!
Marjorie And I've just persuaded Tommy to marry me!
All Hooray!
Squire And if only my wife will let me I'm going to marry Mother Goose.

The Goose chases the Squire off, followed by Mother Goose. There is a general exit as everybody laughs

SPECIALITY DANCE

(*Preferably a number such as "Wedding of the Painted Doll", in which the dancers choreography lends itself to stiff doll-like movements*)

MARCH DOWN

Any suitable march-time number

They march along the rostrum and down the stairs in the following order:—

Choristers
Dancers

Children
Father Christmas
King of Gooseland
Gretchen and Squire Tawdry
Fairy and Demon
Tommy and Marjorie
Willy and Sheriff
Priscilla the Goose
Mother Goose
Jack and Jill

The Fairy and Demon step forward

Fairy To have a happy ending
All Fairy Stories must,
We think the tale of Mother Goose
Is really fair and just.

Demon I did my best to muck it up,
For such was my intention,
But now I'm made redundant
I'll hop off and draw my pension.

Fairy You've said enough "D. Cursemall",
Please cease your silly chortles,
I think it only right
To leave the last words to the mortals.

The Fairy and the Demon fall back into line as Jack comes forward

Jack Oh, thank you Fairy Tinsel,
That's very nice of you,
You've done a really splendid job,
As Fairies always do.
And as a special favour
You've the last line, Mother dear!

Mother Goose What me?
Jack Yes you!
Mother Goose Well, don't be daft,
I'm only here for the beer!

SONG 22

(*This can be a reprise of one of the popular numbers in the production*)

CURTAIN

FURNITURE AND PROPERTY LIST

ACT I

Scene 1

On stage: Village pump
Other village green accessories as desired
Off stage: Throne-chair with poles (**Choristers**)
Long pole (**Tommy, Willy**)
3 golden eggs, increasing in size (**Mother Goose**)
Personal: **Willy:** handkerchief
Jill: crown
Mother Goose: large handkerchief with hole in it
Fairy: wand

Scene 2

On stage: Small counter. *On it:* articles of lingerie, including nylon panties, Union Jack, umbrella (for **Model**)
Personal: **Marjorie:** tape measure

Scene 3

On stage: Trees
Foliage
Large well
Personal: **Mother Goose:** Purse. *In it:* large dummy, large powder puff

ACT II

Scene 1

On stage: Snowman
Off stage: Snowman's eyes, nose, mouth, pom-pom, top hat (**Dancers**)
Sledge (optional) (**Children**)
Pack. *In it:* various presents, sweets, toys, etc. (**Father Christmas**)
Baskets of "snowballs" (**Willy, Sheriff**)
Length of rope (**Demon**)
Lighted candle in candlestick (**Mother Goose**)
Two poles with fake hands attached (**Stage Management**)

Scene 2

On stage: Staircase and rostrum
Golden throne

LIGHTING PLOT

Property fittings required: nil
Various simple settings

ACT I

To open	Full bright exterior lighting	
Cue 1	At the end of final Scene 1 chorus *Fade to* BLACK-OUT	(Page 14)
Cue 2	**Demon** enters *Pick up Demon in red spot*	(Page 15)
Cue 3	**Demon** starts to exit *Flash, followed by white spot on Fairy*	(Page 15)
Cue 4	**Fairy:** "To the Gooseland Boutique!" BLACK-OUT, *followed by general interior lighting as Scene 2 opens*	(Page 16)
Cue 5	**Tommy** exits with **Model** *Fade to* BLACK-OUT	(Page 20)
Cue 6	**Fairy** enters *Bring up white spot on Fairy*	(Page 20)
Cue 7	At end of **Fairy's** song *Fade spot, bring up general exterior lighting as Scene 3 opens*	(Page 21)
Cue 8	As **Mother Goose** stands to go into well *Brief* BLACK-OUT *to cover her exit, then revert to previous lighting*	(Page 26)
Cues 9–12	During Production Number "The Four Seasons" *As each Season starts, lighting change to appropriate quality, at discretion of producer*	(Page 27)
Cue 13	**Kids:** "Daddy! Our new Daddy!" etc. *Fade to* BLACK-OUT	(Page 31)
Cue 14	When **Mother Goose** is in well, and stage is clear *Revert to Lighting as at opening of Scene*	(Page 31)
Cue 15	**Mother Goose:** "It's Priscilla!" *Flash*	(Page 33)

ACT II

To open	Exterior lighting—Snow Mountain—predominantly blue	
Cue 16	At end of Mime and Dance *Reduce blue effect*	(Page 34)

Cue 17	**Mother Goose** and **Squire** exit after duet *Dim general lighting*	(Page 36)
Cue 18	**Demon** enters *Red spot on Demon*	(Page 37)
Cue 19	**Demon** exits, **Fairy** enters *Cross-fade to white spot on Fairy*	(Page 38)
Cue 20	**Fairy** exits *Fade white spot. Bring up general lighting slightly*	(Page 38)
Cue 21	After Skeleton Dance *Dim lighting, shadowy effects*	(Page 39)
Cue 22	**Headless Man** enters *Follow with green spot until exit*	(Page 42)
Cue 23	**Tall Ghost** enters *Follow with green spot*	(Page 43)
Cue 24	General exit *Fade to* BLACK-OUT	(Page 43)
Cue 25	**Demon** enters *Cover with red spot*	(Page 44)
Cue 26	**Fairy** enters *Cross-fade to white spot*	(Page 44)
Cue 27	**Fairy** looks up and points *Bring up full general lighting*	(Page 44)
Cue 28	**Fairy** exits *Fade white spot*	(Page 44)
Cue 29	**Mother Goose**: "My Goose!" *Flash*	(Page 49)
Cue 30	**Fairy** enters *Dim general lighting, bring up red spot on Demon, white spot on Fairy*	(Page 49)
Cue 31	**Demon** exits *Fade red spot*	(Page 50)
Cue 32	**Fairy** exits *Fade white spot, return general lighting to full*	(Page 50)

EFFECTS PLOT

ACT I

| Cue 1 | **Men** charge into cottage with pole
Loud crash | (Page 12) |

ACT II

No cues

Printed in Great Britain by Butler & Tanner Ltd, Frome and London